THE SUMMER OLYMPICS

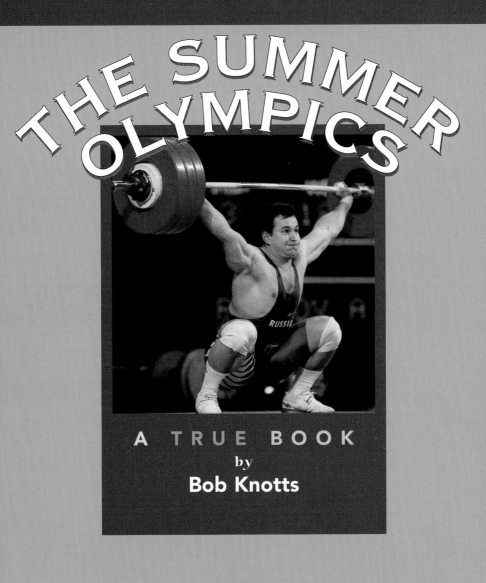

A TRUE BOOK

by
Bob Knotts

Children's Press®
A Division of Grolier Publishing

New York London Hong Kong Sydney
Danbury, Connecticut

A victorious Olympic swimmer

Reading Consultant
Linda Cornwell
*Coordinator of School Quality
and Professional Improvement
Indiana State Teachers
Association*

Author's Dedication:
*To Jill, with appreciation
and love*

*The photo on the cover shows
the Olympic torch during the
1988 Olympic Games in Seoul,
Korea. The photo on the title
page shows a Russian
weightlifter during the 1996
Summer Olympics in Atlanta.*

**Visit Children's Press® on
the Internet at:
http://publishing.grolier.com**

Library of Congress Cataloging-in-Publication Data

Knotts, Bob.
    The Summer Olympics / by Bob Knotts.
        p.   cm.—(True book)
    Includes bibliographical references and index.
    Summary: Describes the history, ideals, events, and heroes of the
Olympic Games, with an emphasis on the Summer Olympics.
    ISBN 0-516-21064-5 (lib. bdg.)   0-516-27029-X (pbk.)
    1. Olympics—History Juvenile literature. 2. Olympic games
(Ancient)—History Juvenile literature. [1. Olympics.] I. Title. II. Series
GV721.5.K57   2000
796.48'09—dc21   99-15090
                                                                    CIP
                                                                    AC

Contents

Olympic runners

What Are the Olympic Games?

Have you ever tried to run faster than someone else? Do you remember how it feels to race against another runner? Or maybe you have watched friends run in a short footrace. The first Olympic athletes ran in races just like that.

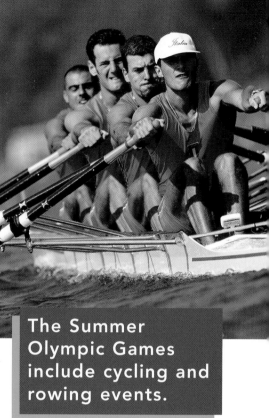

The Summer Olympic Games include cycling and rowing events.

Today, the Olympic Games include much more than footraces. Every four years, the games attract many of the world's greatest athletes. Both men and women compete in the

Olympics. They come from almost every country. They race on foot, in swimming pools, on bicycles, and even in boats. They jump and throw things long distances. They play many types of sports against one another.

Show jumping is one of the equestrian events at the Summer Olympics.

Chinese gymnasts training for the Olympics

The competitors train for years to be the best at their sports. But the Olympic Games do not pay athletes to compete. The winner in each event receives a gold medal as a symbol of victory. The second-

The first-, second-, and third-place teams in a track relay event receive their medals at the 1984 Los Angeles Olympics.

place athlete gets a silver medal. The third-place athlete is given a bronze medal.

No one else wins anything at the Olympics, but most competitors leave the games with

proud, happy memories. Many athletes become close friends during the Olympic Games.

What historians call the Olympian Games began in Olympia, Greece, nearly 2,800 years ago. Only men who spoke Greek could compete in the ancient games.

At first, the only event was a short footrace called a "stadium." Wrestling and jumping were added to the competition by 708 B.C. The discus throw (in which the athlete throws a round disk) and javelin (spear) throw were added too.

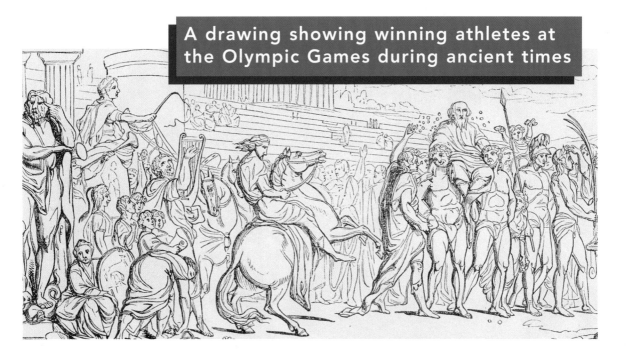

A drawing showing winning athletes at the Olympic Games during ancient times

Centuries later, the Roman Empire won control of the games. Roman emperor Theodosius abolished the Olympics in A.D. 393 after Rome's relations with Greece grew bitter.

In the late 1800s, Pierre de Coubertin, a French baron, dreamed of starting modern Olympic Games to help bring peace to the world. He also hoped to encourage under-standing, friendship, and fair

Pierre de Coubertin (seated at left) was the founder of the modern Olympics.

play. In 1896, his dream came true—the first modern Olympics were held in Athens, Greece.

Since then, the Olympic Games have been held every four years, except during World War I and World War II, when

The first modern Olympic Games were held in 1896 in Athens, Greece.

they were canceled. The Olympic Winter Games were added in 1924, with events such as skiing and skating. The Winter Olympics also are held every four years, but no longer in the same year as the Summer Olympics.

The Olympic Ideals

The Olympic motto is *Citius, Altius, Fortius*, three Latin words meaning "Swifter, Higher, Stronger." These words express the athletic ideals of the Olympics.

But the Olympics are special partly because they are more than just athletic competitions.

German Olympic javelin thrower Silke Renk

The games show how well people from different countries can get along. The Olympic emblem has five colored rings linked together to represent this spirit of goodwill. The rings are blue, yellow, black, green, and red. At least one of these colors is on the flag of each country taking part in the Olympics. The rings also stand for parts of the world—Europe, Asia, Africa, Oceania, and the Americas.

The linked rings of the Olympic emblem represent the Olympic spirit of togetherness and friendship.

The lighting of the Olympic flame during the opening ceremonies of each Olympic Games is always one of the most exciting moments for athletes, spectators, and TV viewers. The flame is lit with a torch that was ignited by the sun's rays at Olympia, Greece. The torch is carried to the Olympics by runners—and by ship or plane when necessary. One lucky runner carries the torch into the Olympic stadium, where athletes will later compete.

The final torch bearer lights the Olympic flame during the opening ceremonies of the 1988 Seoul Olympics.

Let the Games Begin

The Olympics have a creed, or set of ideas, written by Pierre de Coubertin to express the main idea behind Olympic competition. It says that "The most important thing in the Olympic Games is not to win but to take part, just as the most important thing in life is not the triumph

but the struggle. The essential
thing is not to have conquered
but to have fought well."

This means that all Olympic
athletes are winners, whether
they win or lose. It also means

that the same thing is true in everyday life. What matters most is trying hard at something you love to do, even if you fail.

Thousands of athletes compete in every Summer Olympics. Very few win medals

Thousands of athletes take part in every Summer Olympics.

or become famous, but all of them try to do the best they can at their sport.

The Summer Olympics include dozens of sports. Often, many events are happening at the same time in different places.

Track-and-field events are among the most popular sports at the Summer Olympics. Track and field includes many different walking, running, jumping,

The discus throw is one of many Olympic track-and-field events.

The women's 100-meter dash

and throwing contests. Some athletes try to throw things very far, as in the discus or javelin. Others run or walk long distances or make great, long jumps. Still others are sprinters who run short distances very quickly. One of these short races is the 100-meter dash. The winner is called "the world's fastest human."

Some athletes compete in sports that combine several track-and-field events. The hardest of these is the decathlon, a men's event that is made up of ten events. Each athlete in the decathlon must be very good at running, jumping, and throwing. The winner is called "the world's

British Olympic champion Daley Thompson doing the high-jump portion of the decathlon

greatest athlete." Women compete in the heptathlon, a similar competition that has seven events.

The Summer Olympics also have some very familiar sports.

Baseball (above) is a fairly recent addition to the Summer Olympics. Basketball (right) has been an Olympic sport since 1936.

Many are popular games played in schoolyards as well as in huge arenas and stadiums. These include baseball, basketball, soccer, volleyball, field hockey, and tennis. Other Olympic events use bicycles, horses, or boats to see who is the fastest or the best.

Some sports in the Olympics weren't sports at all long ago. Once, they were only ways for people to fight each other. But now they are safe events for athletes, with special rules and equipment. These events include boxing, wrestling, fencing, judo, and taekwondo.

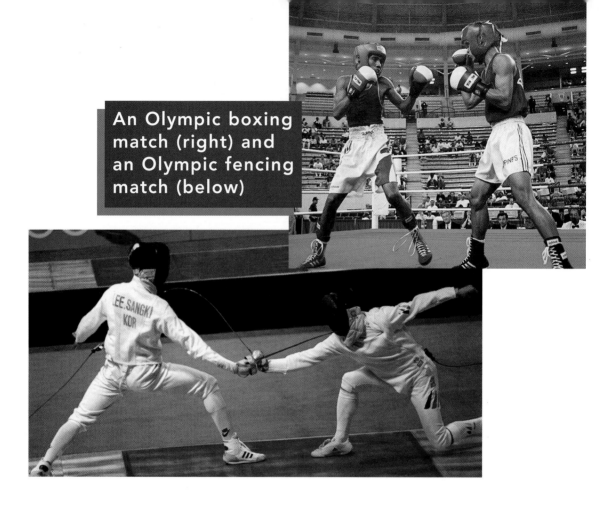

An Olympic boxing match (right) and an Olympic fencing match (below)

In fencing, competitors use swords that have safe, round tips to prevent injuries. Judo and taekwondo are martial arts. Martial arts were invented in

An Olympic
judo match

Asia to help people defend them-
selves against attacks. Today,
athletes in judo or taekwondo
must be careful not to injure their
opponent. To win, they must
throw, wrestle, kick, or punch their
opponent in a safe way.

Olympic

This list shows all the Summer Olympic events—and the year in which each first appeared in the modern Olympics.

Archery: 1972
Badminton: 1992
Baseball: 1992
Basketball: 1936
Boxing: 1904
Canoe/Kayak: 1936
Cycling: 1896
Diving: 1904

Equestrian: 1900
Fencing: 1896
Field Hockey: 1908

Archery

Taekwondo

Table tennis

Field hockey

Events

Gymnastics: 1896
Judo: 1964
Rowing: 1900
Shooting: 1896
Soccer: 1900
Softball: 1996
Swimming: 1896
Table tennis: 1988
Taekwondo: 2000
Team handball: 1936
Tennis: 1896
Track and field: 1896
Volleyball: 1964

Water polo: 1900
Weightlifting: 1896
Wrestling: 1896
Yachting: 1900

Volleyball

Water polo

Yachting

Wrestling

In the Pool and the Gym

Swimming, diving, and gymnastics are among the most exciting sports of the Summer Olympics. Each has many different events, just like track and field.

Swimming and diving take place in a swimming pool. The pool is roped off into eight

The balance beam is one of four women's gymnastics events at the Olympics.

lanes for swimming, with one athlete in each lane. The swimmers race against each other.

Some races are short, some are long. Different races use different types of strokes, or ways of moving through the

An Olympic swimmer doing the backstroke

water. One of these strokes is called the backstroke. The swimmers float on their backs in the water, then kick their feet and paddle their arms as hard as they can.

In diving, athletes make graceful moves in the air while

dropping toward the water. Some divers leap off a wide, solid platform high in the air. Others jump off a springboard, which is springy for extra bounce.

China's Fu Mingxia completing a platform dive during the 1996 Atlanta Olympics

Olympic men's gymnastics is made up of five events, including the rings.

Bouncing high is sometimes part of gymnastics too. Gymnasts must be strong and flexible and must have very good balance. Their routines require creativity and style.

Olympic Heroes

There have been many great Olympic champions. Some competed centuries ago in ancient Greece. Others competed in the modern games.

American swimmer Mark Spitz won nine gold medals. He won seven of them in just one Olympics, in 1972.

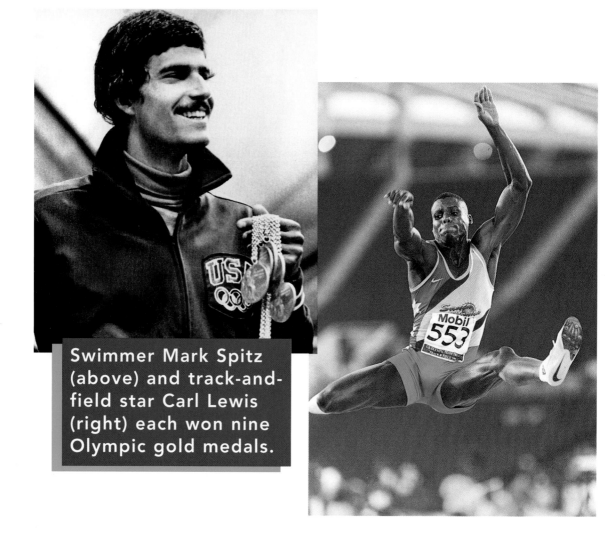

Swimmer Mark Spitz (above) and track-and-field star Carl Lewis (right) each won nine Olympic gold medals.

Track-and-field star Carl Lewis is another American who won nine gold medals.

One of the greatest gymnasts of all time is Nadia Comaneci of Rumania—the first person to earn a perfect 10.0 score in Olympic gymnastics. In the 1976 Olympics, she earned seven perfect scores and three gold medals.

In 1976, Nadia Comaneci became the first Olympic gymnast to score a perfect "10."

But winning isn't the only way to become an Olympic hero. Some athletes must overcome sickness or injuries. Some athletes have little money. Most athletes work hard at their sport for many years to make their country's Olympic team.

This is why everyone who competes in the Olympics is a type of hero. They are people who try hard to do their best at something they love. Pierre de Coubertin knew this is what the Olympics are really all about.

American sprinter Wilma Rudolph (above, right) suffered a paralyzed leg as a child, but overcame it to win three gold medals at the 1960 Rome Olympics.
An Olympic wrestler reacts with emotion to his gold medal win (left).

To Find Out More

Here are some additional resources to help you learn more about the Summer Olympics:

 **Books**

Hunter, Shaun. **Great African-Americans in the Olympics.** Crabtree Publications, 1997.

Kristy, Davida. **Coubertin's Olympics: How the Games Began.** Lerner Publications, 1995.

Perry, Philippa. **Olympic Gold.** World Book, 1996.

Sandelson, Robert. **Ball Sports (Olympic Sports).** Crestwood House, 1991.

Wallechinsky, David. **The Complete Book of the Summer Olympics.** Little, Brown & Co., 1996.

Organizations and Online Sites

International Olympic Committee (IOC)
http://www.olympic.org

This page can tell you about the organization that runs all Olympic Games.

United States Olympic Committee (USOC)
Olympic House
One Olympic Plaza
Colorado Springs, CO
80909-5760
http://www.usoc.org

The United States Olympic Committee supervises Olympic activity for the United States. Its website includes everything you want to know about Olympic sports, past and present.

USA Gymnastics
http://www.usa-gymnastics.org/

A good place to find out more about gymnastics and gymnasts.

USA Track & Field
P.O. Box 120
One RCA Dome, Ste. 140
Indianapolis, IN
46206-0120

USA Track & Field supervises track and field events for United States athletes.

U.S. Swimming, Inc.
One Olympic Plaza
Colorado Springs, CO
80909

U.S. Swimming, Inc. supervises swimming events for United States athletes.

Important Words

abolish to do away with

competition any activity in which someone tries to defeat someone else

encourage to give hope or confidence to

equestrian events various types of horse-back-riding competitions, including jumping over fences

essential extremely important or necessary

ideals goals of perfection

ignited lit

opponent person or team one is competing against

symbol object that represents another thing or idea

Winter Olympics Olympic Games held on ice and snow by skiers, skaters, and sledders

Index

Meet the Author

Bob Knotts is the author of five True Books on Summer Olympic sports. He also writes for national magazines, including *Sports Illustrated, Reader's Digest, Family Circle, Travel & Leisure*, and *USA Weekend*. He has worked as a newspaper reporter as well as in radio and television. He has been nominated twice for the Pulitzer Prize. Mr. Knotts lives with his wife, Jill, near Fort Lauderdale, Florida.